# SUCCESS DECODED

DBEYR – FTC = POV

$$\underline{POV + DILLIGAS + BIO - (2moro + BITD)} = GOWI$$
SH

GOWI + RBTL – TMI (+ WTF) = SUCCESS

NOW, LET'S DECODE THE CODE…

# Table of Contents

# PREAMBLE

I was born in Scotland in 1964, so my childhood covered the 60s and 70s. When I think back, I am struck by the differences between my era and the world in which children grow up today.

When I was young there were no Play Stations, no X-boxes, no internet, no mobile phones, no hand-held computers, no digital or satellite television, no credit or debit cards; we didn't even have a remote control for the T.V. or the C.D. player (oh, and of course we didn't have CDs or DVDs or videos even). In fact, television channels stopped broadcasting at around 11p.m., with BBC1 playing the national anthem.

Indeed, there were only three television stations in the UK at that time and children's programmes were limited to an hour at lunchtime and two hours in the afternoon. I remember the shows I waited for in eager anticipation - the list is endless: Trumpton, Camberwick Green, The Flowerpot Men, The Herbs, Hector's House, Jackanory, Crackerjack, Mr. Benn, Bagpuss, The Double Deckers and my personal favourite, The Banana Splits. And then, as we got a bit older, we watched the delights of The Six Million Dollar Man, Charlie's Angels, The A-Team, Wonder Woman and The Incredible Hulk. Saturday night was all about Bruce Forsyth's Generation Game, New Faces, The Price is Right, the Saturday Night Movie followed by news and then, especially for my Scottish readers, Sportscene with Archie MacPherson. We really lived, didn't we?

And yet, we really **_DID_** live because what we lost in not having modern technology and thousands of television channels and endless hours of mind-numbing American kids' shows, we made up for in our personal freedoms. At only eight or nine years of age I remember a world in which I left my house on Saturdays just as Dickie Davies, with his shock of white hair, was introducing World of Sport on ITV.

My mum would tell me to be careful when crossing the road and off I'd go. I lived in the small town of Prestwick on the west coast of Scotland (about 30 miles south of Glasgow), and my friends and I would gather and run down to the golf course and the beach, exploring local burns, church graveyards, climbing trees, wandering through derelict buildings, shouting at golfers as they addressed the ball on the first tee, and returning home either when it got dark or we got hungry.

Our parents had no way of contacting us, no way of knowing where we might be, and yet trusting our ability to avoid risk and danger. And you know, by and large, we did avoid putting ourselves at risk. Instinctively we knew what to look out for, what to be wary of – we were street-wise and we knew how to keep ourselves safe.

Today, we live in a world that is fearful. Parents have become hugely risk averse, so that their children are exposed to a back garden (under supervision, of course) at best. What really worries me, though, is that children themselves are becoming more and more risk averse. They are surrounded by Play Stations, TVs, computers, the internet, DVDs, CDs, Music

Systems and I-Pods and they communicate with their friends using mobile technology.

When faced with the outdoors children often don't know what to do with it. In my experience, you tell children to go and play in the woods and they are back in ten minutes saying, "We're bored!" Indeed, I have myself heard, "What if there's a bad man in the woods?" How sad that our children have become so fearful. They are now so protected, so surrounded in cotton wool that they are in danger of being unable to assess risk at all. When that happens, and I believe that process has already begun, then our children are in real danger. We risk producing young adults that will be unable to cope with an adult world, either in the workplace or on the street.

So my plea is that each of us is, in some way, responsible for modifying these deep-rooted fears that we all share. We should not place children at *unnecessary* risk but we must expose them to *some* risk. Otherwise, and here is the ultimate irony, we risk their future health and safety.

Being called a name in the playground, being kicked in the shin, being excluded from a group, being made fun of – all of these experiences have happened to us all but in many ways these experiences, in isolation, help us to be prepared for a world where not everyone is kind to us, to a world that does exclude and to a world that will not allow each of us to get our own way. That is not to excuse these events when they occur. However, there are times that we should allow children to fight their own battles before we adults jump in, take over and mediate. If we always fight their battles for them children never learn to overcome problems with others and they become reliant on the adults around them. That is really dangerous – for we risk a world made up of individuals who are fragile beings, incapable of tolerance, compassion or empathy.

Risk aversion also leads schools to remove trees from playgrounds and diving boards from swimming pools. Parents can track teenagers with GPS enhanced mobile phones and monitor their email and phones. Young children have only carefully arranged "play dates".

Do we really have to be so afraid? Is the world more dangerous? Despite the sensational stories in the tabloid media, the answer is probably "no." Reliable statistics are hard to come by, but the risk of abduction seems to have risen at about the rate of population growth for decades and family members commit the vast majority. Physical harm from various activities seems similarly unchanged.

Let's be honest - childhood has never been risk free, but if we succumb to our fears our children may end up ill-equipped to live successfully in adulthood. Protecting children from the risks of tree climbing, swimming pool diving boards, uncomfortable social situations and incomplete homework assignments is almost certain to produce adults with deficits.

When assessing the risks to your child's long-term well-being perhaps the first place to look is in the mirror.

But it's not just parents is it?

The whole of society, certainly in the developed world, has lurched away from personal freedoms and replaced these with a sanitized version of safety to the point where children, and increasingly adults too, operate in a clinical and over-monitored culture. And when a culture focuses on safety and avoidance of risk, our education system and structure reflects those societal pressures.

And this is where I get really interested because I am an educator and I have been teaching children for close on 30 years and I think about the 'art' of teaching almost daily, creating my own philosophy of education that is now at odds with the system of schooling currently being endured by far too many children. We have allowed those in power to create a structure that makes teaching a 'science' and I'll lay my cards on the table right now – that's nonsense. Teaching is not a science, nor is it the province of robotic indifference or deference to higher authorities. Teaching is about relating to human beings and the great teacher is a craftsman who allows creativity and curiosity to flourish; teachers are not just beggared peddlers of information, bereft of personality or ideas.

Throughout my career, I have considered the issue of how to best motivate students. It is clear to me that the motivated, engaged student has considerably improved outcomes later in their student and working lives.

In almost every conversation I have had with an adult regarding their own education, I am always told about the 'inspiring teacher' or 'the teacher that made the difference'. When I first started teaching back in 1989, the teachers around me shared a common view that educating young people was a passion and a joy. I think we are in danger of now seeing education in terms of benchmarks and academic outcomes alone. The education sector in the UK is now quite a stressful environment and when the balance tips in favour of planning, paperwork and assessment, the really vital component of having time to talk to individual pupils on a caring level is in danger of being lost. Time pressure leads to the destabilisation of that very element that should be treasured above all else – the undeniable power of having teachers that are trusted, who treat their students with respect and who have the time to develop the relationship between themselves and their students.

In the final analysis, if there is something in the oft-heard phrase, 'it depends on the teacher', then we should be devoting time to ensuring our teachers and students have a common purpose built on mutual respect and trust. Such a climate should exist and teachers should be encouraged to understand students as individuals. We must be cautious that this focus is not lost in an increasingly competitive and performance-related society.

As Carl Jung said way back in 1954, *'An understanding heart is everything in a teacher and cannot be esteemed highly enough. One looks back in appreciation to the brilliant teachers, but with gratitude to those who touched our human feelings. The curriculum is so much necessary raw material, but warmth is the vital element for the growing plant and for the soul of the child'*.

Wise words indeed.

And when I look back at my own history, I have come to realise that I grew up in a golden age. The 70s were different in a really good way. Parents and families were beginning to reap the rewards of having machines that made their home lives easier, adults were beginning to get more leisure time, families, and in particular children, had considerably more social and personal freedom. It was a period where families, perhaps for the first time since the industrialisation of the world first commenced, were bonded in a way that they had never before been. But, and this is important, parents were still the authority who taught children the difference between right and wrong. My mother and father, Ella and William, lived through the 2nd World War, spending three and a half years apart as my dad endured Dunkirk, the African Campaign, the Italian campaign and finally the liberation of Paris. Once the war was over, they spent the next 60 years providing for their family. They taught value over indulgence, character over celebrity and compassion over greed. And they were not alone. They were carbon copies of families across the developed world that lived and educated their offspring in this way.

I was also exposed to an avant-garde education. This was in the early days of 'open plan' comprehensives, where we all wore white polyester polo necks and fetching purple blazers and where the teachers were either hippies or dyed-in-the-wool dinosaurs. It was a strange mix of people, of methods and of general educational philosophy. As I write this, I'm having one of those 'could that really have happened?' moments, but it really did no matter how bizarre it now seems. Here's how we were taught (and I use that term loosely): we attended school from 9am until 4pm Monday to Friday. At 3pm every Friday we had to write down our 'programme' of work for the following week. The programme was made up of a considerable number of arithmetic exercises, mathematics textbook work, literacy comprehension exercises in the form of colour coded workcards indicating levels of difficulty called the SRA Reading Laboratory, art activities and general topic-based work on nature or history or science or geography. Without a word of a lie, I can tell you now that the teacher did not, at any point in the school year, teach us anything whatsoever. We simply worked our way through the devised programme, corrected our own work as we went (all the books and cards we used had the answers at the back) and no one, as far as I can recall, ever finished the programme. We simply got a new one for the following week, you guessed it, on Friday at 3pm. Our teacher was there to instil a level of discipline and to facilitate our learning when we were 'stuck'. She served no other purpose and she undertook no further roles.

This is a system that should not work. This is a system that appals me every time I think about it, and yet…

In my year group of peers, in this small Scottish town of Prestwick and in this strange educational methodology, there is a high ratio of success – an internationally renowned sculptor and art installation engineer, a lecturer in Artificial Intelligence, a professional golfer, cricketer and basketball player, a leading lawyer for a blue-chip international company, a past editor of the New York Post, numerous doctors and dentists, a deep sea diver, teachers, writers and musicians.

Now, perhaps all year groups are like this but it does strike me that there may have been a fusion between an education system that relied on self-motivation, determination and a degree of self-teaching and a 'golden age' of family and freedom. Was this an age of the perfect mix for childhood? I think it may have been. I discuss this again in the chapter entitled BIO.

Parents today often ask me what the priorities should be within education. I usually remind them of Skinner's quote, that is to say, 'Education is what remains after what has been learned has been forgotten'. This quote makes parents, and teachers too, of course, reflect on what the function of a good school truly is.

When we think back to our own school days, particularly when at primary school, our memories are of those instances when we found something to be funny, challenging or, at worst, humiliating. Today, I believe, the truly successful school is the one that relishes the first two and creates an ethos where the third is unacceptable.

The basis for a sound education has to be fundamentally founded in the notion that learning should be enjoyable and about more than just the simple accumulation of facts. Education intrinsically develops our sprit, our emotional core. As soon as learning becomes tedious or pressured, children switch off completely or become incredibly anxious about their ability to learn. A good education, then, becomes more than just learning for the sake of knowledge. It becomes empowering and creates choice and independence. Learning should be a journey of joy, wonder and excitement. It should lead us into the narrative of our own personal 'success story'.

Education systems across much of the developed world are now so reliant on summative assessment (that is to say, assessment which concentrates on where the children are in relation to curricular knowledge, on a particular day) that the education we truly want for our children is in danger of being lost altogether. We have come to the stage where if we cannot measure something then it is not worth doing and we are the poorer for it. My other major worry is the blinkered belief that the function of school is to teach children *everything*. Our knowledge-based curriculum is becoming so over-crowded that we are in danger of covering everything but doing nothing particularly well.

By de-cluttering the curriculum and by discriminating against continual summative assessment, we free teachers to focus on their own strengths, to take children on voyages of discovery, to allow personal learning and teaching styles to flourish, to remove the pressure that comes from testing and when all of this is allowed to happen, what do you think happens? In the real world, children and teachers begin to truly enjoy the teaching and learning process. We begin again to realize the fundamental need to have fun, to develop a love of learning, to create a nurturing, caring ethos, to support children through their learning.

There are no easy answers but we have to provide an education that is valuable to our pupils, not just for today, but also for thirty or forty years hence. We must ensure that our focus is primarily in helping youngsters to become articulate, literate and numerate but as much as these academic qualities are essential we must go further and ensure that children are being equipped with skills which will allow them to enquire, reflect, problem solve, develop strategies, be analytical and be creative. To do less would be to disadvantage an entire generation.

In addition, we need to think of children as future adults. They are people who will one day lead their nations and it is therefore essential that they learn in a secure environment, where discipline, self-belief and the value of our fellow human beings is central to the learning process. Without developing an ethos where caring for others or valuing differences in culture or religion is seen as worthy, we create citizens who are intolerant and incapable of perspective. This would be the greatest failure of all.

Schools should ensure a strong, values-based ethos where children learn in an environment that is thoughtful and mutually supportive. They must focus on the unquestionable need for literacy and numeracy whilst, at the same time, giving children the breadth and variety of experience that will round them as human beings. We must draw back from the stifling requirements of summative assessment and we must prioritise within our vast knowledge-based curriculum.

Schools develop well when differences are not only tolerated but also welcomed. We live in an age where society, or perhaps government, seeks to ensure 'consistency', but in so doing, parameters are inadvertently set that create a 'one size fits all' mentality. This is dangerous. We need schools to be different from each other; each offering their own priorities and areas of expertise. Why? Because no one system of schooling works for every individual child – we need to address that fact rather than ceding to the belief that education can only be delivered in one way. Standardising education is like suggesting that the fast-food model of takeaway food is an aspiration worth replicating.

No, a 21st century education should take children by the hand and show them the wonder of learning for learning's sake. Standardised education will never achieve that. What we need are schools that replicate Michelin-starred restaurants, each operating to their own standard and to their own priorities. To educate properly we need to care less about the storing of facts and more about the lighting of fires, less about league tables and more about wider achievement, less about examination results and more about the citizens we aspire to be, less about conforming to the norm and more about celebrating differences.

This is the key to societal progress, the key to having an education system that creates the environment and culture for success.

But what about individual success?

How can we achieve that on our own terms? And what does success actually look like? Is it about being famous or being celebrated? I worry that this is the culture that is dominating our students' thoughts today. Youngsters have become so engulfed in the age of celebrity that they truly believe that they are celebrities themselves, inhabiting a virtual world where one's personal remarks, 'likes' and photographs actually 'matter', when the truth is that they don't and not a soul is interested in your night out a week ago last Friday.

They seem to compete with each other gleefully with regard to the number of 'friends' they each have. I know youngsters who are proud to relate that they have "347 friends". I always reply, instantaneously, "No, you don't, you have three."

We seem to have lost our sense of balance, our innate humility giving way to a dark desire to be noticed and celebrated. I am aware, of course, that now that such sites are here, they are here forever. My only hope is that they eventually become the domain of the few and that the majority see them for the waste of time they actually are.

And, in spite of my dislike of social media, I'm going to use the textual acronyms that our young use to create the equation for personal success. Success not in terms of money and celebrity, but success in terms of our personal happiness, security and well-being. Success in our chosen careers and success within our relationships and within our families. Success that is life-long and deeply ingrained. Success where our natural fears and instinctive reticence are replaced with resilience and determination and 'grit'.

And here it is:

$$DBEYR - FTC = POV$$

$$POV + DILLIGAS + BIO - (2moro + BITD) = GOWI$$
$$SH$$

$$GOWI + RBTL - TMI (+ WTF) = SUCCESS$$

Let me explain.

# DBEYR

## (Don't Believe Everything You Read)

"The problem with internet quotes is that you can't always depend on their accuracy" - Abraham Lincoln, 1864

So, 1 type into Google search 'Abraham Lincoln' and 'the internet' and this is the first 'quotation' I found. Now, clearly this is someone's attempt at being funny. You and I can see that without issue. But what about the 12-year-old who has no concept of the world pre-internet. Conceivably, he reads it and says, 'You see, even Lincoln thought you should make sure information is accurate'. Oh, the irony.

There is no question that the internet contains a wealth of valuable content but it can be really difficult, even for the most discerning reader, to separate the real from the artificial. With ease of access, a voracious and infinite readership and zero cost, we can all publish our thoughts, ideas and *facts* on the internet. The Encyclopaedia Britannica can publish online but so too can your twelve-year-old cousin's son of questionable intellect and sanity. And therein lies the difficulty. Who can we trust and of whom should we be suspicious? The reality is that we should be 'critically astute'. In other words, regardless of source, we should question not only the general authenticity of a 'fact', but question who is making the statement of fact, the potential agenda behind making such a statement of fact and whether or not the statement of fact can be backed up by other sources; sources we can, in some way, deem to be reliable.

However, this isn't really big news, is it? We all know that being able to discern what is fact from what is fiction from what is opinion is a much-quoted problem with regard to information found via the internet. And what's this got to do with being successful, anyway?

Well, it's not really the level of accuracy that necessarily concerns me. As we grow older, our experience becomes the ultimate detector of bullshit. But DBEYR is still a serious infringement on our ability to achieve success in whichever arena we seek to excel. The reason I say this is because sometimes it suits us to accept what is written even when we know it's not entirely accurate. We consciously create the mental obstacles to obstruct our progress because we find that more comfortable. We find it easier to choose not to engage than we do to engage and then fail. Our frailty and our innate fear of failure stops us from even entering the race.

Let me give you an example from my own recent experience. As a Headmaster who has been in post for over ten years, I like to keep abreast not only of educational initiatives and development, but also of the personal opportunities which might be available. Occasionally, a post will be advertised that interests me and I will request details of the position. I love reading the glossy brochures which then 'sell' you the school –

the fabulous facilities, the grand traditions, the long and prosperous history, the list of famous former pupils and so on. Then comes the interesting bit – the job description. And this is where our DBEYR demon kicks in. Here is a partial descriptor I was recently sent:

*The following job description is not exhaustive but is intended to give a brief overview of the expectations of the School's Board of Trustees:*

*The Principal will:*

1. Be responsible for the day to day running of the School
2. Chair all senior management and committee meetings
3. Oversee the general sound management of the School
4. Monitor and review staff performance
5. Provide advice and support to the Board of Trustees, staff, parents and pupils
6. Appoint and dismiss staff according to legal principles
7. Ensure sustained recruitment of pupils
8. Ensure appropriate marketing of the school
9. Be highly visible at events, both internal and external
10. Agree and implement the overall planning and development strategy in conjunction with the Board of Trustees
11. Report regularly to the Board of Trustees and its subcommittees providing evidence of impact
12. Be the School's Child Protection Co-coordinator

13. Require to be available to engage in some teaching and cover/supervision duties
14. Meet regularly with senior members of staff to discuss issues pertaining to their specific remits

My DBEYR demon allows me to read the job description but then surreptitiously allows doubt to creep in. This is, after all, a job description for a highly ranked independent school of illustrious and privileged background. Therefore, it is completely accurate. This is what I will be expected to do and to achieve. And then I start re-reading certain words that now jump from the page: responsible, chair, oversee, monitor, review, advise, support, dismiss, ensure, visible, implement, evidence, require, regularly… and almost immediately, I dismiss the idea of applying. Why would I want to leave my job behind when I'm achieving real success here? Why would I want to start again and have to convince people that I am a good leader? This description sounds heavy-handed and dictatorial – I don't think I could work with this Board of Trustees? And what about that term – 'Board of Trustees' – sounds very grand; it's probably filled with stuffy old codgers that wouldn't know a decent education if it slapped them across the face. They won't like me anyway, they'll think I'm not posh enough. They'll hate that I didn't finish University the first time round. They'll realise I'm Scottish and will think that I won't have the right accent for their school. What the Hell am I thinking about? Why did I even ask for this brochure? Who am I trying to kid? Ridiculous idea. And this is the last thought of a 60-second mental tirade before I rip up the description, throw it in the bin at the side of my desk and return to reading an online newspaper. I then spend the next five minutes or so subconsciously deleting the prospect of working elsewhere from my mind.

But let's stop here and analyse what actually happened. The fact of the matter is that I allowed my voice of doubt to succeed. This gets me off the hook, immediately relieves me of the stress of writing an application, attending an interview and being grilled only ultimately to not be offered the position. Actually, the job description is pretty much the same as the one I currently adhere to – the difference is that I am comfortable in my own context. I know all the people I work with, I know all the people I work for, I have established positive relations with all stakeholders in my school's community and the job of leading has become comfortable and yet still challenging. And that's important too. Without challenge, boredom sets in and then we accept change to alleviate boredom rather than seeking change to develop ourselves as people.

When reading that very stark job description I allowed myself to take its contents at face value, without the softening of personal context, but I should have paid attention to DBEYR. The job of Head of School or Principal or Rector is not primarily focused on data and management, it's primarily focused on doing what's right for the students in our care. The person that wrote the job description knows that and so too should the reader.

Remember, the person that wrote the description is selling not only the school but also the perception of a school that is indoctrinated with standards, professionalism and educational proficiency. The writer does not intend to make the school sound cushy, or soft, or comfortable even if the culture and ethos reflects that gentle humanity that exists in many of these institutions.

Our personal voice of doubt is always with us. I wake up each morning in awe that I carry out the work that I do. I often think to myself that this will be the day that I get found out. That actually I'm not that capable, that I do make mistakes and that I'm way out my depth. And then that day finishes and all has been well and the school continues to flourish and my early morning doubts have all but disappeared; only to resurface the following morning. This is the human condition, is it not? To always consider ourselves as outsiders, as not really liked or loved, as inferior in some way to those who inhabit our workplaces. However, in accepting this human condition it would be logical to suppose that everyone has feelings such as these. It would be rational, therefore, to say to ourselves, we all have weaknesses, we all have strengths, but I know myself and I like myself and that is all that is in my power to achieve.

In having a frank and open debate with our own consciousness, we can overcome these very natural instincts of inferiority.

My wife is a teacher too and she is currently teaching 24 nine-year-olds. She discussed with them the idea of internal voices of doubt. She explained how we sometimes believe that people don't actually like us or that we are not very clever or that we are very uncertain and nervous when it comes to learning new things. She asked them to raise their hands if this voice 'dominated' their thoughts relatively regularly. Even she was surprised when 23 hands were raised. But the great thing about that classroom conversation was that it allowed each child to look around and realise they were not alone in doubting themselves. It is this realisation that removes the barrier to our personal success.

So, my advice would be to free yourself of your voice of doubt. You don't need to listen to it. It serves no purpose other than to protect you from the potential pitfall of failure. But failure is not so bad. We've all suffered it, after all. Failure is an essential precursor to success.

Success Criterion 1: Be deaf to the inner voice of doubt and don't believe everything you read.

# FTC

# (Failure To Communicate)

"What we've got here is failure to communicate" – Strother Martin as The Captain, *Cool Hand Luke*, 1967

So, when the Captain utters these infamous words what he is really suggesting is that the repressed and imprisoned Luke is not bending to the will of his authority. It has little to do with miscommunication between the two and a lot to do with the prisoner's belligerence. Little to do with his misunderstanding and a lot to do with him maintaining his personal dignity and upholding an ability to refute and deny a sinister and oppressive leadership.

What this scene sums up is not failure to communicate but rather the difficulty in standing up for a belief or a dogma or a personal viewpoint that is at odds with those in power.

If we remove ourselves from the scripted fantasy of film and consider our place in the real world, our ability to express our opinions and ideas freely is a fundamental right of democracy. However, as individuals, how often do 'we bite our tongue', 'keep our own counsel' or 'avoid confrontation'? There are plenty of occasions when we will have done exactly that and for very good reason. We may not wish to be perceived as bullish or arrogant or dogmatic. We may wish to react in the fullness of time to ensure our emotions are in check. We may not wish to say something which we might later regret. These are all entirely acceptable and natural human reactions. However, what is also clear is that despite a natural reticence to confront, we do oppose and we should oppose when the outcome of such opposition is for the greater good.

There have been countless historical figures who have refused to bend to the will of authority, Martin Luther King and Nelson Mandela being two of the most memorable. Both men stood for what they believed to be right and, in so doing, they have achieved a moral immortality.

I accept that none of us is likely to be the next Mandela, nor do we necessarily need to try to change the world, but at every level there is an important lesson to be learned here. That is to say 'our voice' and the expression of our autonomy is an important facet of achieving success. It is important for our own peace of mind and our own self-worth that we speak up when the need arises or the situation warrants a response that may put as at odds with those around us. In the 21st Century, our failure to communicate traditionally could seriously hamper our ability to succeed. I fear for our young who communicate primarily through media. I love language and the power of words to illuminate and persuade but the advent of the text and of email does impinge on the hugely important nuance of meaning and tone. Had Mandela lived today would he have tweeted his ideas and, if he had done so, would he have achieved the legacy he created? My sense is that his voice would simply be lost in the noise of incessant online chatter. In our own dealings therefore, we need to tread carefully but with determination. We need to build trust by being truthful about what we believe. Politicians today are generally distrusted and the kickback is likely to be severe when the electorate finally gets to grip with the issues surrounding that increasingly national level of distrust. As individuals we need to communicate *consistently* and demonstrate our proficiency and competence. As leaders, we need to go further. We need to express ourselves with passion whilst being precise and specific about our goals or desires.

Success Criterion 2: Failure to Communicate effectively will hamper our ability to succeed in our relationships and in our careers. Our personal satisfaction in doing what we feel to be right cannot be underestimated nor should it be undermined. In other words, stand up and be counted. Do not be afraid to share your ideas and ideals – they matter.

# POV

# (Point Of View)

"The most fatal illusion is the settled point of view. Since life is growth and motion, a fixed point of view kills anybody who has one." Brooks Atkinson, *Once Around The Sun,* 1951

**and**

"O wad some Power the giftie gie us, to see oursels as ithers see us." Robert Burns, *To A Louse,* 1786.

It's a remarkable thing: the human capacity to change and yet, as I explained in a previous chapter, our inner voice of doubt can impact our ability to deliver positive change. Carol Dweck, the Lewis and Virginia Eaton Professor of Psychology at Stanford University, is the expert in this field and her key contribution to social psychology relates to implicit theories of intelligence, described in her 2006 book *Mindset: The New Psychology of Success.* According to Dweck, individuals can be placed on a continuum according to their implicit views of where ability comes from. Some believe their success is based on innate ability; these are said to have a "fixed" theory of intelligence: a fixed mindset. Others, who believe their success is based on hard work, learning, training and doggedness are said to have a "growth" or an "incremental" theory of intelligence: a growth mindset. Individuals may not necessarily be aware of their own mindset, but their mindset can still be discerned based on their behaviour. It is especially evident in their reaction to failure. Fixed-mindset individuals dread failure because it is a negative statement on their basic abilities, while growth mindset individuals don't mind or fear failure as much because they realise their performance can be improved and that learning comes from failure. These two mindsets play an important role in all aspects of a person's life. Dweck argues that the growth mindset will allow a person to live a less stressful and more successful life.

I would encourage everyone to read Dweck's work because it contains hugely important messages about our personal development. The two quotes that I used at the beginning of this chapter reflect those cues which can affect the way in which we operate. We need to be aware of the dangers of the fixed viewpoint – the calamitous effect of being a poor listener, a failure to accept that our point of view is not the only one, nor necessarily the correct one, that we should remain open to new ideas, theories or opinions. That does not mean that our point of view should simply reflect the 'common voice' or that our view should be the most popular of the day, it does mean that we should have the attitude that allows us to question and constantly evaluate our own views. We need to understand that other people's views of us can be important in our own success. The ability to reflect on our words and actions, therefore, is crucial to our personal development and ultimate success.

You know the kind of person I might be painting here – the 'loud mouth', the dogmatic, immoveable bully who never listens to others. The person who blames everyone else for their own lack of success. I am actually thinking of an ex-colleague as I write this, who used to say, 'They're idiots, the lot of them. I've had enough, I'm leaving.' A few months later, in a different educational environment, 'This lot are worse than the last lot – the management team couldn't manage their way out of a paper bag.' What this person failed to realise is that she was the common factor. It did not matter where she worked or, indeed, socialised – everyone else was foolish or inept or poor at their job. The truth was that she allowed her judgement to be clouded and negatively influenced by her own deep-seated lack of faith in her own abilities. Attacking others was a defence mechanism when caught in the spotlight and glare of her own inability. The really worrying aspect of this attitude, however, was that she did not perceive this of herself. As far as I know, she may well be doing and saying exactly the same things now regardless of where she is – indeed, it would be extraordinary if she was not. In other words, she did not 'know herself'.

I have to encourage you to be a person that reflects on 'who' you are. Which aspects of your personality are you disappointed with? Are you too shy, too talkative, too loud, and too critical, are you too prone to putting your foot in it, too complacent, too impatient, and too reactive, too much in a hurry? Are you overly defensive, are you too quick to try to please others, do you compromise when you actually don't want to, are you too angry over issues that don't really matter?

I like to think that we have the ability to go into a darkened room and 'have a word with ourselves' when we get it wrong. However, in my experience, people keep 'reverting to type'. Certain cues trigger a common reaction. I know if I suggest a change to a teaching timetable, for example, that Teacher A will react in a particular way because that teacher ALWAYS reacts in that way to minor change. If you do that, you need to stop doing that. Now.

And this is the whole point of the POV chapter and its beauty lies in its simplicity. Each of us has the immense power to 'decide' to change.

When I was sixteen, and this is absolutely true, I walked into a room of strangers for a social event and felt awkward and out of place. I was ridiculously shy and had always been quite quiet and reserved. It was just my nature. I spent three hours squirming my way around the room, with my head down, avoiding catching people's eyes and, above all, doing anything to avoid being engaged in conversation. Largely, I succeeded, and for all I know, was probably unnoticed by the gathered crowd.

I returned home dispirited and deeply annoyed at my own discomfort.

That night, lying in bed and tormented by the events of the evening, I made a decision. I decided I was no longer going to be shy. I decided I would always look people in the eye. I decided I would engage people I did not know in friendly conversation. I decided that I was going to be a person that people could warm to. I decided to reinvent myself. And I did. The following day I was gregarious, friendly and warm and made a habit of seeking out people who appeared to be uncomfortable in an unfamiliar social setting to put them at their ease.

I like to think I am still that person. And I am that person because that is the person I decided to be.

Success Criterion 3: 'Flip' your thinking and reflect on those aspects of your character that you are less than satisfied with and make the conscious decision to change. That is 'growth' mindset in action.


In addition, this completes the first part of the success code, namely:

DBEYR − FTC = POV

In other words, by being deaf to our fears and removing our failure to communicate effectively, we create a personal point of view that can drive forward our motivation which creates the climate for personal change.

Of course, there's more to success than this simple beginning.

# DILLIGAS

## (Do I Look Like I Give A Shit)

"I have reached a point in life where I feel it is no longer necessary to try and impress anyone. If they like me the way I am, good and if they don't, it's their loss." Corazon Aquino

Terry Wogan, the BBC Broadcaster and presenter, was once heard to say that 'the sooner you understand that some people will like you and some people won't, the better, and that's all there is to it'. He wasn't wrong, was he? No matter how hard we try to win some person over, that person will ultimately decide whether they like you or not and there is actually very little you can do about it.

However, success can never be achieved alone. We all need people around us, whether that be close family members who will do everything in their power to protect you or a loving partner whose loyalty is certain, we all achieve personal success by team effort. So, DILLIGAS actually worries me. The reality is that you should indeed 'give a shit' and that you should also look like you give a shit. As I prefaced this section, you can't win everyone over but you should never give up trying. You should remain loyal to your own personal ideology, remain true to your principles and be a person of conviction and by being that kind of person, one who is true and consistent, we can hope that the perception of us in other people's eyes is increasingly favourable.

If you don't look like the kind of person who genuinely cares what others think then you can't win hearts and minds. The great achievers are passionate about their area of interest, whether that be in the sporting arena, the commercial world or other creative industries. I can't actually think of any world leader, for example, who appears disinterested or dispassionate. Whether that leader is 'good' in all senses of the word is quite another matter but there is little doubt that all leaders are passionate about their position whether because of the power it wields or because of the good their power can bring. Each leader will have their own motivation, no question.

So, what motivates you about success?

I think it might be helpful to view success again in terms of your personal happiness. It is really the centrepoint of the human condition. We need security, we need love and we need sustenance, both physically and spiritually. And when we have those things in place, we can genuinely see our lives as fulfilling and happy. Do you know anyone who feels safe, who feels loved and who is physically and spiritually strong, to be miserable? I don't.

And does anyone who has managed to achieve this state of being look like they don't give a shit? No way.

Success Criterion 4: You have to care. You have to look as if you care. Others around you have to know you care.

# BIO

## (Bring It On)

'Each morning when I open my eyes I say to myself: I, not events, have the power to make me happy or unhappy today. I can choose which it shall be. Yesterday is dead, tomorrow hasn't arrived yet. I have just one day, today, and I'm going to be                    happy                    in                    it.'
Groucho Marx

In my preamble, I wrote a little about my experience in primary school and I want to tell you a little more about it here because I think it's relevant to my thoughts around what makes an individual successful.

I moved to a primary school in Prestwick (a beautiful, small coastal town in the West of Scotland) in 1971 for the start of Primary 3 that was brand new, open plan and a journey into the unknown comprehensive system where we all wore white polo necks and fetching purple blazers, and where we were treated like University students. It was a bizarre experiment where 8-year-olds were given a programme of literacy and numeracy work for the week and where we worked our way through the programme individually and without any teaching input whatsoever. We marked our own work and no one checked to see whether you had completed the programme by the end of the week. Everything I know about education tells me that this system was completely flawed and it should not have worked and yet, in my year group, we have a former editor of the New York Post, a leading internationally-renowned Sculptor, a deep-sea diver who is regarded as being in the top 5 divers in the world, an International Basketball player, a captain of the Scotland cricket team, a former lawyer for a leading computer company, several doctors and dentists, a leading researcher in Artificial Intelligence, numerous self-made business millionaires, two professional golfers and I could go on. It strikes me that this level of success in a single year group is pretty odd. The only answers I can come up with are that:

- we were given responsibility for our own learning
- we became competitive with each other in completing tasks
- we developed a work ethic and a can-do attitude
- we weren't spoon-fed or overloaded with boring, secretarial work tasks that had little educational benefit
- we had freedom to explore our own understanding and the opportunity to experience our own personal successes.
- I am not suggesting that we follow the system but I do think each of us can learn lessons from it.
- As individuals:
- we need to hand much more responsibility for learning

on to our own shoulders
- we need to have high expectations of our own abilities and our own limitless potential
- we need to allow ourselves to be increasingly creative
- we need to access opportunities for philosophical debate and argument
- we need to be self-motivated.

Education currently focuses on knowledge acquisition which is then tested against an examination system that provides a national, standardized benchmark. That's all well and good but that's really about management of data at the expense of improved performance. I have never believed that intelligence is fixed or that we are pre-disposed to a certain future on the basis of our academic ability. For me, having been in classrooms for 30 years, students are all capable of learning. The process of becoming educated, however, should not merely rest with the single objective of knowledge acquisition, thereby proving ourselves to be intelligent in that very narrow, academic sense. Education's primary concern should be in producing young people who are cultured, empathetic and responsible.

To be successful, therefore, is not actually about proving oneself academically. To be successful, you need to prove yourself as a 'human' being. In other words, the key to success is your determination to have a strongly-developed work ethic and to be respectful and show kindness to your peers. Kindness is often overlooked and we need much more of it.

Success Criterion 5: I like the BIO strand - BRING IT ON! Don't be resistant to change or afraid of altering direction, be energized by it. Take charge of your destiny – that does not mean that we should pursue control of everything that happens in our lives, the more we try to do that the more likely we are to lose control. No, focus on the day ahead; and as Groucho said, 'be happy in it'. Work hard, be kind. It's a really simple way of getting through each day. And if you REALLY DO that each day, well, your future is assured.

# 2moro + BITD

# (Tomorrow and Back In The Day)

'The struggle you're in today is developing the strength you need for tomorrow.' Robert Tew

**and**

'I really don't think in the past. I sit down with my friends at dinner, and they like to talk about the good old days. I'm respectful of the good old days, but I find myself spending very little time reminiscing. I'm really looking forward.' Donald Bren

Tomorrow:

It's an interesting word, isn't it? It conjures up so many connotations and can sometimes paralyse us with inactivity. I remember coming up with a phrase when I was a student that seemed to amuse my more hard-working peers. It was, 'never do today what you can put off until tomorrow'. I lived by that for three years and got precisely nowhere. Three months away from my final examinations at University, and in my final year,

I quit. I walked away from University much to the bemusement of my family and, particularly, to my mother. She couldn't quite believe that I was giving up so soon to the final goal of achieving my degree. What she didn't realise was that I had given up long before. I had hardly attended in that final year and I had no chance of passing any exam. The truth was I had kept on thinking that 'I would do it tomorrow'. Oops.

And that's what I mean by saying paralysed by inactivity. I allowed myself the comfort of idleness because, let's face it, not having much on your to do list is really quite nice. I liked being able to 'laze', watch television, visit friends, lunch in the park, enjoy the ambience of my local drinking establishment, philosophise endlessly in meaningless conversations and then return home for more television and, as a direct result, always later to bed than was ever genuinely healthy. A late night meant a late rise which meant I'd missed the first lecture of the day – 'not much point in going in now. I'll make sure I get in tomorrow'. And so on, ad nauseum. Tomorrow became a fiction but that gave me the satisfaction and, indeed, the certain knowledge that everything would change the next day. But when the next day came, it was literally 'today' again and again I allowed my lack of drive to consider that 'tomorrow' would be the better option. So, in essence, what you must say to yourself is 'don't put off until tomorrow what you can do today'. That simple semantic change is like a light bulb moment. If you keep that principle to the forefront of your mind everything changes. Your life becomes dynamic and you find yourself energised way beyond your wildest imaginings. Try it.

Do everything you need to do, and that you can do, today. I can assure you that years of putting things off on a daily basis leads only to boredom and a lack of direction. It leads to a sense of uselessness and a tendency to think in terms of 'what's the point?' Being active, taking the bull by the horns and completing tasks ahead of time feeds the human soul. As the well-known ad makes reference, 'Just Do It'.

Of course, tomorrow can have another very demoralizing and de-energising influence upon us. We cannot control the work ethic and dependability of others. How often have we heard, 'Yes, I'm on it – I'll get it to you by tomorrow at the latest.'? I've heard it regularly and whilst on many occasions tomorrow comes on time, there have also been plenty of occasions where tomorrow has meant two to three weeks later. In other words, our own inertia can be created by the lack of productivity of those around us. How do we cope with that irritation? Not easily is the true answer. That is why it is so important that when viewing our own success that we do not blame others for our failure. I tend to see others' inertia as their issue alone. I can only concentrate on my own level of enthusiasm, passion and drive. Whilst I can encourage those around me to be similarly positive, I can't force anyone to be as productive as their potential allows. I can only work on my own potential.

The message here is actually a relatively simple one. Always outperform your own view of your potential. Sometimes if we concentrate on achieving more than we set out to do, we become liberated by it. For example, I set myself a target of 200 words a day writing this book. I think that is a sustainable number that allows me to concentrate fully on the content without becoming diverted by other tasks to be completed. In other words, that number is achievable on a regular, daily basis. However, after three chapters, I was achieving 500 words a day. This was hugely liberating because it gave me the impetus to keep going at a higher rate than I had originally considered to be my potential. In essence, I was outperforming my potential. The goal, which is completion of this book, gets ever nearer as a result of ever-increasing productivity and the sense of satisfaction that brings about is tangible. And, it feels good!

Back in the Day:

Of course, the direct opposite of tomorrow is yesterday and part of the human condition is that we are forever looking backwards. Now, that is obviously hugely important. We all know that our history, both personal and in the wider context of society as a whole, informs our future. Or, at least, it's meant to. We do learn from past mistakes even though the doomsayers like to encourage us to believe that we don't.

If you consider society as a whole then our current circumstances are infinitely superior to those of our forefathers. There are many who say the world is a more complicated place, that we have too much reliance on technology, that we are harming our planet, that we risk losing species because of our mismanagement of natural resources, that the human race is unnecessarily selfish and that we are walking towards self-destruction. On many levels, all of that may well be true but, as individuals, we can only do that which lies within our direct power to influence. Do not get bogged down by the bigger picture – start small, concentrate on making your life the best it can be and do likewise for those around you: for your family, your friends, your neighbours and colleagues and then look to assisting your local community. I liken personal influence to the ripple effect in water. What starts with the dropping of a pebble creates wave after wave. We can do likewise but only if we start with ourselves. We, alone, can't solve the problems of the world but we can fix our own.

The reasons for believing the modern world is superior to that which our ancestors endured are numerous: advances in personal health, hygiene and medicine, improvement in communication and transport networks, the consistent availability of food and water, the care we give to our young and to our elderly. One hundred and fifty years ago, it was not uncommon for children to live on the streets of slum cities, gambling, smoking and drinking. It was not uncommon for these same children to be put to work in factories or in 'sweeping chimneys'. We've come a long way in reality. And we've done that thanks to individual people working initially on themselves and then spreading out their ambition and desire for societal improvements to others. Our influence can actually know no bounds.

Success Criterion 6: So whilst tomorrow does indeed come, we should not ignore our past. We should be prepared to learn lessons from our mistakes and not to be overly defensive when we make them. Hold your hands up and say 'yes, I'm sorry, I got that wrong' – it actually feels great when you admit to a failure. Don't allow yourself to be paralysed by inertia. Outperform your potential. Don't look back and be overly nostalgic – instead look back and see how far you've come. And then, push on. Not just for yourself but for those around you. And let that number be ever-increasing. Never lose sight of the fact that our success is only meaningful if we touch the lives of others in positive and rewarding ways.

# SH

# (Shit Happens)

"The pessimist reasons that things just happen, where the optimist believes that things happen for a reason." Anthony Liccione

In 1989, I was a Housemaster in a boarding Prep school in Ayrshire – sadly no longer in existence (not my fault...honestly). It was my responsibility to look after 20 boarding children from the end of the school day at 5.30 p.m. until assembly the following morning at 8.40 a.m. Fortunately, I was young and did not really take the responsibility too seriously. The great thing about being young is that you tend to have suffered fewer disasters than those older than you. I think it's called 'the innocence of youth' or something. Anyway, my educational life had yet to be blighted by disaster and therefore my time as a Housemaster was generally worry-free. However, this honeymoon period did not last beyond my second term in charge of the boarding house – I was the only member of staff living in the main school with the children, by the way. The Headmaster and Deputy Head had houses on the Estate and could be called in an emergency.

It was a bleak, dark, cold and damp February evening. I headed off to bed at around midnight having checked that the boarders were all asleep and that the burglar alarm was set. I was looking after my parents' young collie pup and he had been walked and was happy to settle down for his night's sleep too.

At around 1 a.m., I woke up to the sound of a distant bell. It was probably the worst time of the night or day for a bell to sound as I was in the deepest sleep ever and was only minutely aware that something was not quite right. After a good five minutes of coming in and out of sleep, I realised to my horror that what I was hearing was the Fire Alarm sounding. In a second's passing my responsibilities struck me and I leapt out of my bed shouting various expletives whilst trying to coordinate my body into achieving the impossible task of putting on a dressing gown. No easy task in complete darkness and with the brain blurred and dulled by a heavy sleep.

I hurtled towards the flat's front door, considering as I went the possibility that the children had already been fried to a crisp whilst I had happily ignored the bell in favour of a couple of more snores. Of course, at this crucial moment, I had entirely forgotten the fact that I was also looking after Corrie, my parents' pup. Unlike me, she had heard the bell and had been so frightened by its siren that she had emptied the entire contents of her lower bowel on to the hall carpet. My right foot, unslippered and therefore entirely bare, met with this less than desirable pile even before my hand reached for the doorknob which would have lead me to the dormitory block.

So, I have yet to get out of my flat, the fire alarm is blaring, the dog has expunged all over the carpet and my foot is now covered in excrement. Not a great start to the 'saving lives' part of my job description. The dog is barking loudly and I am now hopping on my 'good foot' wondering what my next move should be. And this is when genius struck. I hopped into my bathroom, shoved my 'crappy' foot down the toilet and flushed. This cleared the main area of debris from my foot and I was able, finally, to hobble out of the flat, ready now to be heroic.

I can't quite remember why I then failed to go to the dormitories. I think I had taken so long to get out of my flat that I assumed, naturally, that the children had managed to get themselves downstairs and out to the fire assembly point in the school's front porch. Instead of heading to the dormitories therefore, I turned to my immediate right, which would lead me downstairs. What I forgot was that by opening the door to those stairs the burglar alarm would also sound!

Taking the scene as a whole, then – the dog is going mad and barking ferociously, the fire alarm is sounding, the burglar alarm is also sounding, I've still got traces of dog faeces on my foot and I've yet to spot any children.

As I reach the bottom of the stairs, I am met by the Headmaster, fully dressed in a suit and standing looking at me with his hands on his hips (It transpired that he had been woken by the alarm too, even though he was 300 metres away in his bungalow, had got up, got dressed and walked up to the school in the time that it had taken me to meet him half way down the stairs from my flat).

'Ah, Mr. Grant; how nice of you to make an appearance.' He said this whilst quizzically looking at my right foot, which I was still holding off the ground in a somewhat eccentric manner. 'Just out of interest, where are the children?'

My brain was still muddled and so I mumbled feebly, 'Are they not in the front porch, then?'

'No, I don't believe so. Perhaps you might like to find them and follow our fire alarm routine – you know the one – where we save the children from the inferno like we're supposed to.'

The sarcasm was lost on me at that precise moment. I ran back up the stairs, gathered the children and brought them down, where we followed the protocol by taking a roll call.

Unfortunately, the Headmaster hadn't finished with me. 'Am I right in thinking, Mr. Grant, that the burglar alarm is sounding too?'

I smiled and laughed one of those nervous little laughs. 'I think that was me coming down the stairs.'

He looked at me blankly before drawing out an extraordinarily long, yet cutting, 'Yes…'

Once both alarms had been switched off and reset, I took the children back to their dormitories. I was not in the happiest state of mind as the Head had just told me that he wanted a 'little chat' with me the following morning. Little chats were neither little nor chatty in my experience. Anyway, I took this opportunity to get tetchy with the children. 'Why on earth didn't you get up and go downstairs when you heard the alarm?'

One wee brave soul then informed me that the Head Boy, also in a state of delirium, had told everyone to go back to sleep because Mr. Grant had everything under control. I couldn't help but see the irony in that.

So, why am I telling you this story? Well, no matter where we are or who we are or what we are doing, shit happens. Sometimes, in such situations, we have a tendency to be self-defensive and to make excuses for things that have gone wrong. In my experience, the best way to approach your own mistakes is to admit to them openly. 'I'm sorry but this is completely my fault' or words to that effect. It has a remarkably calming effect, both on our own state of mind but also in the state of mind of the person who is asking what went wrong. As individuals and as a society, we see failure or making mistakes as a calamity to be avoided at all costs. We live in a world that automatically points the finger of blame. We live in a world that is, perhaps, somewhat less forgiving than used to be the case.

And yet admitting fault is immensely liberating - even when every instinct and sinew in our body is telling us to divert attention away from our own errors. Try it the next time something goes wrong. Put your hands up and say, 'That was my fault. I got that terribly wrong and I'm sorry.' In most scenarios, our mistakes are less important than we believe them to be at the time. Being open to mistakes, indeed embracing them, allows us to learn.

Success Criterion 7: We all make mistakes. Admit them. Reflect upon them. Learn from them. Success is bred from learning from our errors.

This also completes the next part of the success code. Having created a personal point of view that drives forward our motivation and nurtures a climate for personal change, we now focus on the perception that we create in others. We need to care but we need also to look as if we care. Take charge of your destiny, be energised. Don't wait until tomorrow. Do it today. Do it now. And don't let the everyday 'shit' get in your way. Don't look at life as a series of obstacles to overcome, rather be creative and motivated by your inner belief. Confidence is inside you – don't hide it, don't be afraid of it, celebrate your potential. Doing all of this brings us to the conclusion of this part of the equation – GOWI. In other words, don't procrastinate, don't listen to your voice of doubt and insecurity. Just 'Get On With It' – what the hell is stopping you?

# GOWI

## (Get On With It)

"Man often becomes what he believes himself to be. If I keep on saying to myself that I cannot do a certain thing, it is possible that I may end by really becoming incapable of doing it. On the contrary, if I have the belief that I can do it, I shall surely acquire the capacity to do it even if I may not have it at the beginning." Mahatma Gandhi

**and**

"All our dreams can come true if we have the courage to pursue them." Walt Disney

If you're anything like me, you probably sit watching television and listening to political debate without having anything heavy nearby lest you throw it at the TV in utter frustration. How many times do you hear politicians go on and on and on about the need for reform or change or divergence or convergence? The debate can last for months, sometimes years, and I find myself shouting, 'Shut up and just get on with it!' usually with the odd expletive thrown in for good measure. Nothing frustrates me more than incessant talk about change without any change taking place whatsoever.

Do not allow yourself to be bogged down in detail and wordiness. Structured and well thought-through plans are, of course, essential, but how often do we come back to acting on our instinct? I think we should listen to our 'gut' a lot more often and be prepared to act quickly and decisively and with conviction on changes that we want to make in our own lives. Procrastination actually leads to inaction which actually leads to constancy and constancy is the enemy of progress. Personal success derives from reflecting on where we are and determining where we want to be.

1. Evaluate the situation
2. Reflect on the aspect of your life you wish to improve
3. Plan a series of actions that will lead to change
4. Act
5. Back to point 1 (evaluate your new situation etc.…)

The process of change is, I conclude, cyclical in nature. We should never stop trying to achieve improvement. We don't jump the train. We stay on our journey and go through our series of evaluations, reflections and actions. By the way, that doesn't mean we never get off the train and change direction.

Let me give you an example from the world of education. Much of the developed world now focuses on attainment almost solely in schools. I have long argued that this system leads to pressure which impinges rather than enhances our learning. However, the powers that be tend to do more of something similar in order to create a different result. They are then confused when their minimal 'tinkering' doesn't make a blind bit of difference. I liken western education to everyone being on a large boat. We are all on it – governments, public officials, educators, pupils, parents and we're all trying to go along with the perceived wisdom of the day. The problem is that the boat is heading for Antarctica and what is required is the steering to be ever so slightly turned in favour of sunnier climes.

You may think you are on the right track. Everyone around you might think you are on the right track but if the track doesn't lead you into the success you are trying to achieve then don't be afraid to change your mind or alter your direction of travel. Think about destination. Think about sunshine and warmth and feeling good. If your current journey isn't making you feel that way, put the brakes on and turn your wheel.

And we shouldn't, as I have said before, shy away from failure. For me, what defines us is the manner in which we succeed, the manner in which we fail and the manner in which we conduct ourselves in the world in which we live. The highest compliment we can ever receive is that we handle success and failure in precisely the same manner. That our reaction to each of those radically different outcomes should be indiscernible, that the outcome, good or bad, should be handled in precisely the same manner: with good grace, with dignity and with humility. Each of us is a winner and each of is a failure. Accepting that fact creates balance in our lives and allows us to see the bigger picture.

One of the most important attributes a person can display is that of resilience. Resilience is now considered by many to be the greatest single indicator of a person's future success. Too many people do not try to succeed because they are frightened by the potential to fail. When we receive a knock, when we encounter an obstacle we should not shy away or seek the comfort and help of others who we deem to be stronger; we should stand proud and be prepared to acknowledge that the biggest failure of all is to have never tried to succeed.

And there is an important message for us all in this. We must be able to accept failure, to accept coming second, first or last. That we can accept being left out or included because the world now expects nothing less from its citizens but a sense of humility, dignity and resilience. If we continually crumble at the first sign of difficulty, or at those events which scar us emotionally, we are destined to fail.

The most successful people in life are not necessarily those who are deemed the most intelligent or the most academic. The true success stories in history are of those people who are committed to a cause, who have a strong work ethic, who are determined to succeed and who are only spurred on by failure; people who, in essence and to their very core, believe in themselves.

Success Criterion 8: Don't shy away from your insecurities and your fear of failure – be energised by it, confront your fears head on, don't procrastinate. Believe in yourself. Make the plan and continually re-evaluate where you're at. Decide what it is that you are going to do and get on with it!

# RBTL

## (Read Between The Lines)

"Opportunity is missed by most people because it is dressed in overalls and looks like work." Thomas A Edison

I've been teaching for almost 30 years and in that time I've come across tens of thousands of students. I've listened to their dreams, their fears, their misconceptions and their 'voices of doubt'. I've done what I can to furnish them with sound advice. As I look back, I get the privilege of hearing the success stories. Unfortunately, I also get to hear of stories where the outcomes are less than rosy.

There seems to me to be a pattern, and whilst all generalisations *are* wrong, there is something I want to share with you that you may find of benefit. The ability to achieve success or experience failure seems to me to have very little to do with academic ability or academic intelligence or lack thereof.

Finding success seems to be a lot to do with seeing opportunity and grasping it. Indeed, not just 'seeing' opportunity but 'actively' looking for it. The entrepreneurs that I come across in my work all have resilience, grit and determination in common.

And they have all – every single one of them – experienced failure, often multiple failures. Did those failures stop them from searching other opportunities? No, they did not.

No matter how many times you fall, get up and start again.

As Sinatra sings, in 'That's Life', he is 'Riding high in April, Shot down in May' and 'Each time I find myself flat on my face, I pick myself up and get back in the race.' And later in the lyric, and sounding somewhat clichéd, my favourite part of the song, 'I thought of quitting baby, But my heart just ain't gonna buy it…'

That is the essence of success. It doesn't come to those who wait, or to those who dream, it comes to those that do. I am talking here, of course, primarily in terms of career success. You work for a long time in this world, so make sure it's something you really want to do, that you are passionate about and that keeps you energised. And, if you find yourself in work that does not promote those positive feelings, leave it behind. And yes, I know that's a risk. But better taking the risk then living an unfulfilled life.

I remember early in my career hearing a story from a retiring Head Teacher which has remained with me throughout my career. He talked of a time twenty or so years after the end of World War 2 when he was starting out. His first appointment was as a teacher in a small boarding school in the South of England. He had been there for less than a year when during morning break on a sunny May morning, the Classics teacher, a military type, stood up from his chair and bellowed to the assembled staff members, 'Righto, I'm off!' before proceeding to the coat stand, taking his coat from the peg and placing a black trilby on his head. The staff room fell utterly silent as no one really knew what the gentleman actually meant.

The Headmaster, also from a military background, stood up. 'What do you mean, old fellow? You're off?'

'Indeed, Headmaster.' The elderly gentlemen looked around at the puzzled faces of the other teachers. 'You see, my friends, they've become the enemy. And that's not right, is it.' He was, as it turns out, talking of his pupils. He could no longer see the good in them, he only saw that which displeased him. He recognised that fact and acted upon it.

You have to admire that level of self-knowledge, the ability to see his own fault and his determination to do something about it. Apparently, so the story goes, he did indeed march straight out of the school's front door, walked down the main driveway and was never seen or heard of again. But I'd be willing to bet that his life improved. I'm also willing to bet that so too did the life of his pupils.

If you're not happy, change. We all have a right to happiness and it's out there for each of us. Go and find it, even if you need to 'read between the lines'.

Success Criterion 9: What do I actually mean by that? Well, often, the picture is unclear and we are not certain of the right route. We try things and they might not work out. Whatever it is that you do, make sure the subtleties of disharmony or dissatisfaction are not missed in the busy bustle of your life. I think too often we are deaf to our own desires and needs. They can seem unattainable or fanciful but our dreams should never be that. Grasp the nettle. Do what feels right. Seek happiness. Look for clues in your everyday life that make you feel fulfilled and concentrate on them. Life is great – concentrate on and develop the good stuff. And when you see it going badly wrong, like that Classics teacher did, have the strength of your conviction and leave that disillusionment behind. Being unfulfilled has no place in your life so don't let it ever take hold.

# TMI

## (Too Much Information)

"When the world throws you too much information, the only way you can stay sane or survive is to look for pattern recognition. Amidst all the blurs, is there a constellation that emerges, is there a straight line that's emerging?" Douglas Coupland

I really like this quote. It sums up succinctly the problem with information overload and how practically to overcome it. It goes back to my earlier point about gut instinct. Through everything that life throws at you are you able to see the 'stars' of opportunity? Are you able to tell the good from the bad, the important from the trivial, the inspiring from the demotivating?

See yourself as a compass set to follow that which magnetises you, interests you or sparks your thinking.

Karl Fisch in his short film 'Shift Happens' describes in brilliant detail how the world is changing and the struggle we often have to keep up. My favourite 'fact' from that video is the snapshot regarding information overload in the 21st Century:

*'It is estimated that a week's worth of the New York Times contains more information than a person was likely to come across in a lifetime in the 18th Century'.*

Makes you think, doesn't it? What information do we hold on to and which information do we jettison?

A whole lot of questions.

So what are the answers?

Well, let's be honest here. Let's be critically astute. The actual fact of the matter is that we, as individuals, are more than capable of sifting through the information that is thrown at us daily and dealing with it swiftly and competently. I don't buy into the idea that we are indiscriminate in our interests or in those areas which awaken our natural curiosity. We are actually adept at information gathering and we're getting ever better at it. We know what we like, and equally, we are aware of when we are being 'sold' an idea. We are not just brainless automatons sleep-walking into a desolate future.

Discerning the quality from the quantity is becoming one of the most important skills for today. Taking that which informs our future and ignoring that which is merely 'chatter'.

C. Wright Mills, an early social scientist, adopted the theory of the social imagination, this being the ability for a person to place their personal problems in a framework of social issues that affected them. Mills suggested that, 'What people need is a quality of mind that will help them to use information and to develop reason in order to achieve lucid summations of what is going on in the world and of what may be happening within themselves. The sociological imagination enables its possessor to understand the larger historical scene in terms of its meaning for the inner life and the external career of a variety of individuals.'

That's academic-speak, isn't it? What it actually means is that each of us is able to pigeon-hole information. We understand our own life and our own desires and we can place these against a wider societal context. In doing this, we develop our understanding. We are conscious beings after all, capable of considered thought and action.

So, what does this all mean for us in the context of our lives? The reason I was keen on including a chapter regarding the vast quantities of information available to us is actually quite a simple idea. What I suggest is that you don't worry about 'not knowing enough'. The whole point is that we can't know everything, that we'll never know everything. We need to be guided by our inner convictions and take the information that is available to develop our own personal understanding.

Success Criterion 10: Don't be anxious about that which you do not know. Focus on those areas which interest you. Don't be frightened by your lack of experience. Develop your experience over time. In other words, accept your knowledge limitations and do not use these limitations as an excuse for inertia.

# WTF

# (What The F**k)

"When a person thinks that everything is going wrong, something wonderful happens in his life." Dalai Lama

I once knew a person who, when describing a leak in her shower, said, 'Why do bad things happen to good people?'

Wow.

The same person sent me the following text massage: 'Am I working too hard? Yes. Have I taken on too much? Yes. Has it taken its toll on me? Yes.'

That was it. I read it with bemusement and wanted to release a deep sigh. How does one respond to a message like that? Well, I'll leave that to your imagination.

I know countless people who view themselves as victims. Victims of unfortunate events, victims of others' mistakes, victims of bad luck, victims of a million other things. None of us can get anywhere in this life if we view ourselves, our decisions, our actions in such a negative, glass half-empty way.

The last piece of advice I can give you, therefore, is to steer clear of the victim mentality. As I said earlier, shit happens.

Deal with it. Don't look for the wider implications. Don't consider that the cosmos is conspiring against you, expunge those ideas relating to 'bad luck'. Accept that things go wrong. After all, failure is success if we learn from it.

One final analogy for you. Early in my teaching career, I taught a boy who was gifted both academically and in sport. He had everything going for him. Later in his educational career, at a different school, he suffered a lengthy period of ill-health just at the time he was preparing for the crucial examinations that would unlock the door to University. The pressure of being unwell, combined with the difficulty of just being a teenager, combined with the importance attached to his exams lead him into a nervous breakdown from which it took over a decade to fully recover. He never sat the exams, he didn't go to University and he suffered from bouts of depression.

I met up with him and because he loved golf I tried to think of a way of bringing that game into developing a way forward for him; a new mindset, if you like. I wanted him to know that there is always light at the end of the tunnel.

I spoke with him at length, and I have used the same story I told him in countless assemblies with children ever since. I hope it unlocks something in your own limitless potential.

When you play golf, no matter if you're a rank amateur or a hardened, competitive professional, the aim is simple. You hit a small, usually white, ball off a small tee towards a distant flag. The object of the game is to get the ball into the hole at the base of the flag. Everyone's objective is the same. Imagine yourself on a one-hole course. You're standing on an elevated tee and the flag is 450 yards away. You strike the ball in the direction of the flag and attempt to avoid obstacles that may be in the way – trees, bushes, bunkers of sand or water hazards. You might do brilliantly and get the ball in the hole in two shots. You may have a disaster and take seven shots. It may be the first time you've tried to reach any golf flag and it may take you even more strokes. The point is that if you keep aiming for the flag, your ball will eventually reach it. It might take two shots. It could conceivably take 200 shots. However, if you persevere and keep aiming for the flag, you will get there.

You WILL get there. Guaranteed. It would defy all the laws of the Universe if the ball were never to reach the hole.

Your life is like that too. If you have a goal in mind, you will achieve it if you keep aiming for it. Some people will find that journey easy and will reach their goal quickly. Some will struggle with obstacles and hazards and poor stroke play and will find the journey long, hard and difficult. But if your aim is kept sure, you WILL reach your goal.

Of course, I can't end the WTF chapter without recounting one final true story that proves, beyond any doubt whatsoever, that anything can happen. An event that you could never plan for and never be prepared for. The secret to our success lies, not necessarily in our planning or on our readiness for all eventualities, but on the understanding that we will all encounter WTF moments. It is *how* we react that determines the final outcome.

I've always secretly admired those teachers (and Head Teachers and Principals, in particular) who bounce out of beds in the morning, go for a cycle, a swim, a 3km run and appear at school by 7.30 a.m. full of energy and endless enthusiasm and optimism for the day ahead. I have a tendency to hit snooze repeatedly before falling out of bed and heading bleary-eyed towards school – a short 200 metre walk away from my front door – arriving slightly behind my start time of 7.45 a.m.

Anyway, all of this by way of introduction to me being woken at about 7.35 a.m. by one of the wide-awake type, my Primary 1 teacher, Miss Kell. The immediate thought that runs through my mind when the phone rings at this ungodly hour is one of despondency as I recognise the likelihood that it is a member of staff who is unable to come into school that day. However, on this particular morning, that was not the case.

'Hello?' in the most polite tone I could muster.

'Ah, good morning, Headmaster. Rachel here.'

'Morning, Rachel. How can I help?'

'Just thought you might like to know that there are four bulls walking up the school drive, Headmaster. Slightly concerned that this might worry a few of the parents as they drop their kids off.'

At this point in the conversation, as you may imagine, my first thoughts are possible newspaper headlines should the said bulls prove less than amenable to hundreds of children running at them and poking them in their eyes, ribs, rump and so on and so forth.

After a lengthy pause, therefore, 'Mm. I see. Well, thanks for letting me know. I'll deal with it.' Looking back, this last sentence seems somewhat ludicrous in its simplicity. Somewhat understating the enormity of the number of potential problems that could by incurred by four bulls wandering aimlessly around the school playground.

However, no point in getting into a panic.

I got dressed a little too hastily for comfort and made my way (ran in a non-panicky type of way) down to the school. There were, indeed, four bulls, now standing on the front lawn eyeing cars and children suspiciously.

I decided the best approach would be to stand between the bulls and the arriving parents/children and do my utmost to make light of it all. So there I stood, smiling, waving and acknowledging the parents in a kind of 'Isn't this just the funniest thing?' kind of way.

Brian, our Estates Manager, appeared. 'You've spotted the bulls then,' in his usual understated manner. Indeed, I had noticed the bulls. I was more worried that they had noticed me and that they were summing me up in a very disparaging and slightly worrying way.

'Where in Hell's name did they appear from?'

'It's a long story...' I had thought it might be. 'Well, they belong to a local farmer who has been trying to track them down. They've been on the run for the past three days.' At this point I had a vision of them in masks running from the law.

'They nearly had them last night but the police arrived with flashing lights and their siren blaring and they legged it.'

I've never been able to work out why police use their siren in situations that clearly require a sense of decorum and quiet order. Then again, perhaps they wanted the bulls to leg it.

'Anyway, I've phoned the farmer and he's coming out with his team to re-capture them. They're bringing a very large cow. Apparently, she'll be able to herd them.' It didn't really give me a considerable sense of relief to learn of this plan. However, I became distracted by a lunatic member of our parent body, who had decided, in a moment of blinding stupidity, to take flash photographs of the four beasts.

'Brian?'

'Yes, headmaster?'

'What the bloody hell is that crazy woman up to now?'

Brian shook his head. 'I think she's taking photographs…' At which point the bulls took an unhealthy interest in her and started walking towards her.

'Brian, there's about to be bloodshed.'

The bulls had now gathered momentum and the unfortunate parent had taken refuge in one of our more prickly hedges in an altogether unflattering and undignified manner. At least she would live. In my somewhat agitated state, I did wonder whether or not this could be considered a positive outcome.

However, my priority was to put all the children's minds at rest and so I continued to smile and casually saunter around the

71

lawn. By the time the farmer arrived the children were safely ensconced in their classrooms and the potential for disaster had all but been entirely negated.

So, there we have it. A quite remarkable event that no Head Teacher or Principal or Director would ever assume might happen during the normal routine of the job of running a school. But it did happen. And that's the lesson to remember. Regardless of who we are or on what stage of the journey we are on, you just can't account for those WTF moments!

Success Criterion 11: Keep focused on your goals. Don't lose sight of them. Keep aiming and don't give up because it gets too hard. Stay positive; don't be a victim. And, regardless of how well you understand the previous 10 success criteria, expect the unexpected!


Yes, we're nearly at the end.

GOWI + RBTL – TMI (+WTF) = SUCCESS

Get on with it but don't be afraid to change direction if it 'feels' right to do so. That does not mean stop. That means change direction but continue to travel to a new goal, to a new destination. It doesn't mean get off the track and sit in the waiting room. Don't expect to know everything. Remember, no one knows everything. Stay focused, stay true, stay determined.


Success is just around the corner.

# SUCCESS

## (SUCCESS)

"Success is not final, failure is not fatal: it is the courage to continue that counts." Winston Churchill.


I want to finish by really repeating the success criteria we have studied through the course of the Success Code.

1. We all have an inner voice of doubt. DO NOT LISTEN TO IT.
2. Have CONVICTION in your thoughts and about your ideas and passions.
3. DECIDE to change those aspects of your character or personality that you are dissatisfied with.
4. CARE.
5. Work hard, be kind.
6. Admit to your mistakes. Don't be paralysed by inertia.
7. View your mistakes as learning episodes.
8. Don't procrastinate. BELIEVE in yourself.
9. Change direction if you need to, but DO NOT STOP.
10. Don't be concerned with knowing EVERYTHING. You can't; neither can anyone else.

11. Keep your goals strongly in your focus (whilst appreciating that anything can happen along the way…)

And, from me to you, I wish you all the very best in pursuit of your dreams. You are a precious individual, capable of greatness and with a limitless potential. Now, go out and do it and don't look back.

Printed in Poland
by Amazon Fulfillment
Poland Sp. z o.o., Wrocław